Lost Stations

– Stride –

*for my family
far and near*

LOST STATIONS

Jennie Fontana

LOST STATIONS
First edition 1995
© Jennie Fontana

ISBN 1 873012 89 6

Cover art © Pamela Doran
Design by Joe Pieczenko

22/5/96

Acknowledgements
FatChance, Foolscap, The North, Orbis,
Poetry Australia, Poetry London Newsletter,
Poetry Wales, The Rialto, In the Gold of Flesh
(The Womens' Press), *Klaonica: poems for Bosnia*
(Bloodaxe Books).

'In the Mariazell Chapel' was a runner-up
in the 1991 Bridport Poetry Competition.
'Lost Stations' won 2nd prize
in the 1991 'Time for Verse' competition,
and was broadcast on BBC Radio 4.
'Over the Bar Into the Deben' won 1st prize in
The Battle of Maldon Millenium Competition.

The last three lines and title
'Throwing the Lightness on These Things'
is from Joni Mitchell's album *Court and Spark*.

Published by
Stride Publications
11 Sylvan Road, Exeter
Devon EX4 6EW

Contents

3. C'era Una Volta

1. Lost Stations

FIRST BORN

it was not the way I'd planned it
no rhythmic pants
between the pushes
and you wiping my brow

just a numb trickle
of being and a silence
as they sucked her out
and wrapped her in
the white sheet

left alone in the dark
I lifted her small
shocked body into my bed –
close and afraid
should I wake her

MUTE

the trumpet player
practices scales

notes blurt and spit
out of his open window

behind thick nets
the woman practices motherhood

through chinks a semblance of tune
climbs into her lap

starts her swaying
sets a foot tapping

then stumbles
leaves her clinging

bold cries cleaving
her closed skull

BLOOD SPORT

dialling home
hoping my fingers connect
baby daughter paced through
the night crying
feeding crying

the front door closes her father
to work

out in the wild bleaks of Essex
with no washing machine
and the privy on the edge of the field
your hand felt frost on the quilt
in the morning

you snatched me
off my tartan rug on the slope
under the tree
out of the tracks of the hunt
that split over the garden
kicking my toys

it was hard
and I know

I can hear a bark
a gritted white howl
and the tally ho
of expectations –
pinks flashing
in the distant woods

I'm sitting on a threadbare rug
under a stark tree

I feel the drum
of hooves
skinning the ground

I hear the click
of the phone
the click of
the kitchen latch

you leave me frozen and
reeking of fox

LOST STATIONS

They took you of the incubator:
dressed and tucked you into
a clear-sided open cot in a cubicle
down the end of the corridor.

A bonnet on your head
to keep the heat in:
your tiny wrist name-tagged
and a thread of plastic tubing
snaking out of your nostril,
held against your cheek
with snips of sticky tape.
You were always asleep.

They chained a black radio
to the creaking radiator:
fluorescent hospital initials
would glow their daubed identity
in the dark.
Each time I came – at 6 at 12
at 6 at 10 at 6 o'clock –
they'd turned it on again.

But the tuning had always slipped
and it would be fuzzing its lost stations
scrambling and scraping the intentioned soothing
company of voices and music.

I would turn it off.

ON LEVEL 14

the crane is hoisting the next piece
it flutters
slung in chain
belying weight
at this height

the wind always blows up here
squeezing cries down clogged shafts

when it hurricanes
power fails and
nurses hand-pump air
into ventilated babies

gulls hold wings
against the blue
and dip each blast

way way below the sea
moves scratching surf
along the strobed length of pier
glinting its mirrored ball
and veining horror's eye with
the red-watted octopus ride
spinning out over the end –

the cordonned beaches are
patrolled by silent hoverers
as cyanide cylinders
roll in on the tide

AT THE PIT

this mother sits on a bench
she watches sand spill
into her children

her hands flick ash
lift a plastic cup of scummy tea
to drained lips

behind her
boys on the high ramp
roll on skateboards

hands push air aside
wheels run
knees ease
into the crouch –

she registers the roll
and slap on the ply bank
but thinks thunder
and moves to go

the children chewing sand
and fag-ends wail
as her chapped hands
smudge their smiles

she lifts
bending a spine
curved into clearing babies from the womb
(a coccyx shattered
by the final push)
humped over buggies
down basement steps
stooped over faceless mouths

at soured breasts –
cringed round a husband
who wakes her for his share

she crouches
into a ball
the smallest thing
she can be
bent round the ravelling coil
turned into the spring –
her final pounce

OVER THE BAR INTO THE DEBEN

High tide for the don't-knows
attempting to align this meted course
with the wind touching eight
against us

vomitting into this narrow-necked river
waves mash on shoals

we hug the steep beach where Martellos
stark the wall
poke Peggotty chimneys into
the fouled sky

the sounder bleeps us round
bleeps the shifting shingle bar that
maps can't mark –
we're running out of water

frozen with sick spilled on your hand

my hand wrapped thudding the flinging rope
someone is notching a winch –
snared sail smacks ears dead

the lifebelt lifts and hits her snatching
tissues over their heads the gimballed
pan of rice upturns below –
we throw sea into the cockpit

tack for the opposite shore
where missiles fill the tree line

FLOWERS FOR SYLVIA
Heptonstall, April 1988

without my babies
they see straight through me
on my way to the churchyard

your name painted
black one-brush strokes
on a triangle of
random stone

flowers for Sylvia
"from Richard"
it said on the
florist's card
crocuses
and jasmine
in a jam jar
droop

you before me
we walk

past chimneys
and arches
and bridges
down the Calder
where water drips

tree roots round iron

cornerstones that tumble
motionless down the valley

a twiggy nest ungainly
in the fork of a branch

blue enamel spatter
of a smashed egg
clean in a niche –
I touch a tiny piece

depressed steps and paths
straight down the hillside

the stones laid neat
edge to edge
without mortar

a single crowfoot
closed
cold
against the wall

POOL CAFE
(for Mary)

like ex-lovers we sat
coffee filtering into our cups
you were shadowed by bruised days

I wanted to breathe you awake
shake the warm blood back

on the gradual steps of the learner pool
a woman leaves her crutches on the side
her friend holds her

the blue water laps the weight
lifts her lost limbs
spreads them into a star

fingertips slide over palms
their grip slips
and they smile as she
floats alone

EYE OF THE HURRICANE

you came
like a dream

blue eye
of the hurricane

and sowed seeds
of infidelity

you stripped
to the waist
and cleared
our garden
with my husband

I watched you
stack fallen creepers
and dead leaves
and cover them
with earth – to rot

pick flown slates
and broken glass
and tuck them safely
from the children

you hitched a strong
rope and shackle
round the storm torn
cherry tree
and pulled
it down

my daughter my son
poked woodlice

out of the dusty core

we watched them

"You have beautiful
children. You have
love," he said.

you came
like an angel
out of the hurricane
and turned my eyes
to the salt
catching sun
on my windows

DAUGHTER

I swing you
"Higher, higher."
you demand,
"higher than Robert!
As high as the sky!"

you must be higher

I used to push
and 'boo' and
grin full-face
as you came back to my
outstretched arms

tickle your
little socked feet
that had buffetted my womb
less than a year before

but now your long legs
in patent shoes
kick sharp and with a thrust
apart from playful

warning off
kick out and back
with a drive that brings
the secret pattern
that swings you
without me

MY DAUGHTER'S FIRST STILETTOS

Holding the door frame you teeter
out over the threshold. Arches taut
testing the water, an angel's foot
stepping out of heaven.

Your white socked toes claw the ground.
You're learning to capture an audience
with the snare drum of heels,
snagging invisible nets as a mermaid's fin.

It was the same for me with my mother's only pair –
black pointy ones, with cold silver tips to the heels,
that I scraped along the side path one hot Sunday
between our yellow brick garage and next door,

from the dustbins to the front drive.
Up and down, up and down the side path all day –
snaring ears.

But I cannot deny you your stiletto heels:
the delight in scratching sparks,
perfecting the potential to pock magnificent floors.

FULL LENGTH MIRROR

Your parents' house was the only one I knew
with a full length mirror. Coming downstairs
I'd get a really good look at myself.

When they were away you let me
have their double bed.
Your boyfriend was smaller than mine.
We were both on the pill and sex was easier
than a top-of-the-43-bus-Peter-Styvesant –
after all we always ran the risk
of getting caught – exhaling.
They must have smelt the smoke.

Divorced you arrive with your son,
holding flowers and presents for the new baby –
sweets for the children.
A day between our birthdays kept us closer
with news twice a year. "Hope you're all
well and happy" I wrote – August '87
and you rang, simply said she was dead.
Your parents had taken her to the beach.
Air sea rescue found her body.

Our giggling surprises me –
your daughter's ghost
easy between us
as we prepare fish fingers, chips and ice cream.

I show you around:
I have a full length mirror
in my daughter's room.

I have a stripped and unwanted mantelpiece
and you need one.
We carry it out to your hatchback.

The back seat is stiff –
it hasn't been lowered before.
We almost rip the head-lining as we wedge it in
but can't close the door –
so decide to saw it in half
but then can't get it out.

We cry with laughter –
uncontrollable on the pavement
holding each other.
Just like the night
when there were six of us in a Fiat 500
on our way to another pub
and we got stopped by the police –
who then escorted us home.

IN THE MARIAZELL CHAPEL
within the Monastery Precincts of St. Peter's, Salzburg

This place is for serious prayer, closing
at 5.30, as we enter. The old monk gently
teeters a brass snuffer to each of the six creamy white
candles on the gold, emblazoned Rococo altar behind
the rood grille. Cherubs pout and angels pose: some cover
their breasts, coy, with only wings; some avert their eyes.

A tiny crowned virgin hovers centre stage: her dot eyes
lost against the frills of crinoline and ruffles closing
around her neck, full and wide so as to cover
all of her: no legs, and where her arm should be gently
cradling, a baby sticks out like Punch and Judy's. Behind
a red velvet veil, the sacrament; the altar cloth, white.

Under a single chandelier: iced floral twists, white
drops and cascades, silvering light – we stand. Our eyes
follow this frail, black cassocked man. He comes from behind
the grille: an expert at unlocking, opening and closing
the gate silently. He kneels: his head bowed gently,
his child-like black boots have no cover.

A novice enters: his sandals sport a lack of cover,
for his socks, startling under black, are pure white.
He is carrying a green plastic watering can. Gently
he waits, ready to receive the key: their eyes
meet and he bows. Unlocking the gate, and closing,
he goes in, stretching to water the altar flowers behind.

But he cannot reach and so, without a look behind,
this blond youth folds back the crisp, lace edged cover,
precisely. He lifts himself onto the altar and kneels, closing
our focus in as he then kicks off his sandals to stand, white
socked, moving the candlesticks to expose the vases. Our eyes
can only watch, ears listen to, the water trickling gently.

His task complete he lowers himself gently
down, replacing each thing as it was: gilded shafts behind
point every item into place, along with sandals. His eyes
lowered with his exit, and his bow; a signed cross to cover
him. He smiles, with his green watering can and white
socks. We smile, and turn, knowing this is now closing.

He follows us gently as if to cover
our steps from behind. He turns off the intricate white
light. Our eyes adjust to day while the door is closing.

IN THE BOAT YARD

It was later when bathing us she'd said,
"Don't touch yourself there.
Don't let anyone touch you, there."
that we told her.

In the boat yard where the Blackwater licks
up and down the slipway
where boats are hoisted out for winter
their high hulls chocked up with tree trunks.
We played there, my sister and I
and kids from the other boats, mooching about
while our parents, angling blow lamps,
dragged and stuttered triangular scrapers
at gummy swaths of anti-fouling.

We played between the tarred sheds
poking at lidless paint tins
loving the puckering skins
and especially the piercing
when the residue oozed through
and we'd use it to daub
something anything anywhere
with a stick or stiff dead brush.

In windcheaters and boots
we played along the cat walk
stilted in fascinating mud
that popped at low tide.
We rarely went to the end
where barges and motor torpedoes
were undergoing endless conversions
littering the decks with half sawn sheets of ply
and discarded dog houses.

We made each other walk the plank

across squidgy black ponds in the marsh
that only flooded on high water springs.

One Saturday I left you behind
while I went up to the town to buy sweets
with the blond boy.

Left behind
and alone

always curious to see
the inside of another boat
a man we knew from around the yard
invited you into his cruddy smack
at the end of the cat walk.

I know you'd remember the sweets
I brought you back from the town:
colourful acid-drop beads –
mouthfuls tipped from the white paper bag
to the final trickle of dusty sugar
we'd sometimes choke on –
I've forgotten their names.

THE OLD SUMMERHOUSE
(for Katie)

Fidgetting to share secrets
we walk across the fields
from the long house you are building.
My daughter joins us –
dances almost under your feet.
Borrowed boots drag my steps
but I catch up as she starts
to taunt you with a daring balance
on rickety planks across the stream.

We walk through the abandoned tannery
past reedy drained lagoons
where they used to rinse hides.
She finds the stickiest mud
weighting the bottom of her boots
so that they fall off.
We have to stop and clean them
banging one each
echoey in the yard amongst empty sheds.

The locals have told you
of teas at the manor house
and fêtes on the lawns.

We know it was beautiful –
the octagonal summerhouse
built around a tree that's grown
and shifted the walls.
A canopy of permanent shade
that nurtures moss and lichen.
Red and blue glazed panels with cut stars
tilted by a floor of roots –
not one is smashed.

When we were small
we would have had this
as our perfect house:
with plates and cups and food and beds
where we would live forever
and do our washing in the stream.
But you wait by the gate
while Josie and I step in.

GOING TO BUY A CAT FLAP IN DIEPPE

You wavered
but I'd done French at school.
"Une flap pour la chat" – easy – "s'il vous plait."

I'd forgotten that five years of it at the Comp.
had made Miss Armstrong cry.
Her high pitched Scottish accent
freckled our vocabularies.

I'd sat with Paul Godwin.
My mother'd hit the roof of her Mini
when her headlights caught our first kiss
after the Friday night disco.

There were no regrets even when exposed
in backstreet hardware stores
gesticulating the movement
of the flap swinging thisway-thatway

confidently imitating the common
multi-national sound for a cat
to overalled assistants behind long counters.
"Bonjour. Voulez vous? Au revoir. Pardon?"

You still remind me of this
especially when we have visitors
and more recently
when you talk with the children.

We left with an oversize stainless steel
pressure cooker for my mother
tied in brown paper with string.
She put it on the bottom shelf in the pantry.

It has never been used.

2. Red Pretender

BLACK DOGS

Remembering those black dogs
he'd sent pencilled onto A4,

she was mauled by their audacity:
peeled lips and grim growls.

In dreams they slid over the brow
of a hill and skulked to the kerbside.

Grey light blurred shape and number
but their presence tightened her.

Now, after patient months of food
and outstretched hands; avoiding sudden moves;

taking care to nullify frowns; clearing
her voice of fear and aggression –

they lay quietly. She dares to believe that
they are guarding every corner of her:

raising their lids when hinged doors flap
and loose boards rock, knocking pipes.

Ready to impale intruders, she thinks,
with their ignited eyes and eye teeth.

LEARNING THE ROPES

She watches it dock
the China Ship with the dragon
carved on its prow.
It brushes the butterfly tree
bursting from the green-blocked
walls of the river.

She is not the French Lieutenant's
shawled woman hazed with storm
or the ginned body swollen with the tide.
She waits for the Captain,

paces the 'Marble Quay' a hundred years before
the anchored ache of phones;
before the sheathing of disease
and babies.

He stills the wheel and shows her
how to slip the rope and knot it
round the boomed slack of sail
to stop it billowing.
She learns to cleat the sheets
and coil them flat on the deck.

She takes him to his quarters
where they can hear the winding winches
and drop of sacks into deep holds
through the open windows.

He gives her oriental boxes
of lacquer and jade and silk
carved and painted and woven
with dragons and flowers
and wild horses.
They are fastened with

bone pegs that push through loops.
"Open them when I'm gone,"
he says.

She sits on the water-stairs
and watches the sails hoist
on the China Ship.
As she waves he can see
the green bangle on her wrist.
He takes the wheel and she catches the wind.

AT THE POOL

holding her weight
like a water-winged baby
he rocks her in the shallows

her head tucked on his shoulder
he scans the steps for other high-thighs
and licks chlorine from her neck

the whistle blows and
the lifeguard points at
the indiscretion

so he swims her to the deep end
lifts her out then
lets her slip from the side
into the splash between his arms

his hand on her head he
pushes her down

THE GRAVEDIGGER'S ORCHARD

It is not marked on the map
this orchard shaped as a half-closed eye
between fields on the ridge of the hill
where the track hairpins.
The footpath runs close
but folk avoid the gravedigger's patch
as they do the hangman's.
I know this earth –
the sweat of layers beneath the topsoil
to water
to rock.

I have pushed the hawthorn to a weave
that keeps out all the bitter winds.
The apple trees have flourished
from those first seeds –
Discovery.
I have kept them low
we need no ladders come harvest
the long grass cushions the windfalls
there is little bruising.
I know you can see their red blush
from your attic window.

When the wheat's as golden as our child's hair
light the copper
wash the patched white linen sheet.
I will watch for it
scooping the breeze on your line,

watch you gather it
breasting its span
stretching your arms to form
an enormous butterfly.

When everyone sleeps
and the orange moon has almost set
you come with this tight folded whiteness
clutched to your belly
stepping the path between the rasp of crickets
and the rustling of ready grain.

Together we stretch the corners
between the trees –
lay back so the fruit falls
into our palms.

Soon we will plant a walnut sapling.
When our skin is as crumpled as the inner shells
and our hands can only hold each other
its wood will make a fine table
for the boy to polish.

THE GRAVEDIGGER'S WIFE

tidies her childless days
her ample hands twiddling threads
into lace
patterning pins
in the red velvet cushion
rattling the beaded bobbins
clicking the light
through their glass eyes
of fire water sunshine ice

she fiddles at lengths of trimmings
for christening gowns
collars and cuffs for Sunday dresses
an ornate shawl to tuck
where a neckline leaves the flesh too bare
veils in black and white

heirlooms

the women of the village prize
these floral drizzles

she likes to think of her handiwork
close to their skin
weighting their petticoats
girdling thighs
flouncing young breasts

she likes to think of handiwork
being ruffled by men

THE GRAVEDIGGER'S LOVER

grates the soap
into the wash
tastes its dust
in the rising steam
her cheeks reddening

still close to birth
the child
pulls himself up
into the mass of her skirts
presses the crown of his head
between her legs
the fabric resisting
as a hymen before breaking

she wipes her hands
over milk-sore breasts
cups his head
and the hair feels just as his father's
when she strokes him

all evening
every evening
with a sock and darning wool
snagging in her chaffed hands
until the lamp flickers soot
with no stitch sewn
the hours nicked with the sound of her husband
splitting logs for the winter
his simple blade unfailing
thud thud
stacking the wood by the wall
he does not see his debris in the dusk

she dreams her lover

is in the bed
while her husband is sleeping
naked she rolls and rolls with him
he inside her and the baby
tumbling between them
laughing
like a small bell in a rattle

every morning she sweeps splinters
from the path
the barefooted child on her hip

THE BLIND EYE

the blind eye
turned in
gawping
through cracks
in the heart

MARY'S PONDERINGS

"But Mary kept all these things,
and pondered them in her heart."
Luke 2.19

ponder these things in my heart
gob-smacked more like
highly favoured
inhabited by the Holy Ghost
beware girls
bloody wonderful it is
and there's no precaution
to block out such love seeds
stashed full of Cupid's arrows
little barbs that embed in the womb
brings you to shouting his name
out loud
every time
so's the neighbours would hear

these brief visits
while the baby sleeps
and Joseph out planing wood
up to his ankles in shavings –
fleeting as the glow
on a blown out candle
aching for the flame
God, this is love

never saying what I really want to say
all the bloody time
wanting you to see this child growing
to hold him
me
to know the joy
of his small hand
his laughter

every day something new –
to wake in your arms

God, this is love
all this pondering
while you're busy spiriting other women
sending in the angels
with all their unflappable surety
whispering inside their heads
"fear not
fear not"
over-shadowing

God, this is love
Joseph adoring this child
coming home arms open
lifting him over his head
gabbling their little nonsense
and me tapping food
onto our plates
slicing the bread

if I were to say
"Look Joseph dear Joseph
I'm really sorry but
you're not his father
God is"
that would be cruel
he would never feel able
to keep our bed warm
to cherish us
he'd have nowhere to go
he might want to know intimacies
might want to hit him
would sense everything in his broken heart
might turn us out
me out

might leave the child
fatherless
motherless
God, this is love

THE MONTHLY HOUSE
AT HELLBRUNN

loose from the stays
sore to the touch I pull off
leave him clouded in curls
run in my cotton shift
through neat gardens wetted by fountains
spilling centres of symmetry
fly stone steps two at a time
leave the palace far below
for my turretted haven
cupped by mountain and pitched forest

the key turned ready with the moon
I burst in blessing the dark
press my belly on the stone floor –
they leave my food at the door
but no one enters

I pelt walls with ink
bang windows with shuttered poems
hole stones with black eyes
and rat them down cellar steps
dislocate bats from my hair

I roll in my skinned bed
with curdled dreams
stab the fire with rusted swords
and rip rags ready
for the bleed

RED PRETENDER

"a few little goodies for Grandma"
she says giving me the basket
making me wear that wretched
itchy red cloak with the ties that rasp
at my chin more irritating than hair
down the neck after a trim
she made it out of a pair of Dad's old trousers
found the pattern in some yellowed 'Woman's Weekly'
so pleased with herself for being so clever
economising and aspiring to haute couture
stepping back and smoothing my shoulders
"It suits you – red
gives you a healthy glow"
as if I was sickly without it

and then the jolly wave from the door
all the way down the garden path
and the blown kiss and "Bye darling"
when I get to the gate

am I glad when I get round the bends
of the wood and the path darkens
I've got better things to do
with my time than fussing with Grannies

she'll be snoring
breaths of death that fill the room
I'll tug her arm
and say in my syrup voice
"Dodo dear Dodo
(that's what we call her)
look what I've brought for you"
and she'll be all dribbly
and I'll wipe her mouth
while she tries to name me

shunt the pillows up behind her
sit her up

find her glasses on the table
amongst the sagging fruit
bitten biscuits
brown bottles of pills and
milk of magnesia all runny
crusted down the blue glass
spoons dimmed with it
say "there there"
put the basket beside her

she'll get out her paper
and the fondants
while I hold my nose
empty the commode
retch
disinfect
done!

then I go round the back
under the lean-to
where the mossy logs are stacked

he's always there
all over hairy
sparkling teeth
coal-pit eyes

I let him undo
the bow at my neck
(can't wait to get it off)
he licks me
nips

when its really cold

49

he carries me in
we put Dodo in the cupboard
with her paper and a brandy
we growl in her bed

sometimes we pretend he's a Granny
and I'm the nurse
sometimes
he's as hungry as a wolf
says that he's going to eat me
stops the scream in my mouth
with his long tongue

CHARMER

See these fingers that flutter
as if stretched into
the sterile snap of rubber:
with these I wave the thicket aside
for you to step into
my clearing.

At dusk I draw a hoop in the dust
with the index finger of my left hand.
You will remain in this circular space –
moving only when I say.

You will hear no one calling your name.
You will never feel the same, again.

Between chat I slip old spells:
'my dear',
'between you, me and the gatepost',
'in complete confidence',
'you can tell me'.

You barely notice the casting
that releases your dry tongue
and secrets.

I finger them in the cleft of night
until they glisten.
Charms on my bony blue-veined wrist
hooked into a time-worn chain –
jangling with every move I care to make.

Kept under the pulled cuff of my sleeve
I will show them to whoever I please.

DENT IN THE WALL

I.

Unmoulded. Barely uncurled. Knew only
the clamp of lips round rubber teat
filling mouth with milk and her own
sounds when cold leaked.
Cries hammered on ear-skins
sealing sharp words – shaping night-space
startling emptiness – arms fight din
reflex shudders – crumple face.
Stuffed with wet wheeling dark
movements rumble swinging light.
Shuddered whites lock the look
up up as if they might...
       wrap and hold
       the limp shell.

          *

II.

They never knew the clenched squeal
of laughing body – fists unfolding
as small hands – large hands – feel
the warmth of touch moulding.
Feet dancing on thighs pushing out
the boundaries of a tiny world:
the sucked satin edge of comfort
shredded and discoloured as it's unfurled.
They only knew the numbness
of 'giro' waiting: forty dragging fags a day
and sex,
grudging anything that blocked their way.
A need to make their mark: the unknitted skull
perfectly matched the dent in the wall.

TOM THUMB & THE WOMAN WITH THE SILVER CROSS

I have you safe now Tom Thumb
my sweet one that came tumbling out of a pucker
in the skewed satin edge of my blue Whitney blanket
that morning after he'd gone to work

all those years pinching
for the slack elastic of mucus
taking my temperature –
plotting his entries with precision

each season marked with the renewal
of ribbons in bootees –
the fluffing and refolding of terries
pulling the Silver Cross
carriage pram out of the shed
vacuuming the hood and interior
the once-over with Milton
the impregnated wadding I rubbed up the spokes
thumbed round the wheel rims before T-cutting the body

it would stand in the hallway
where the low sun made ruby light
through the stained glass front door
making it glow –
when he came home from the office
he had to scrape past it

until I found you
scooped you into a scratch mit
amongst the layette I packed in the pram
the blue blanket holding everything in
I backed out and up the crazy path
past rose bushes and lime-trees pruned into stumps
walked down the hill towards the glinting sea

I have kept you away from the meningitis
from the dangerous kitchens and ponds the stairways and hinges
crowded places where you might tip into some ample pocket
where untrained hands might mash you
not knowing what you are – not knowing
the importance of keeping their fingernails short

deep in the arches of railways and piers
I nestle you warm as a turd
sing you the songs about blue boys and sheep
twinkle stars and bye-buntings in skins

3. C'era Una Volta

CARLO

(who died in the DC10 crash
outside Paris, 3 March 1974)

It was negligence –
no peephole
to check
that the bolt
had gone home.

Your mother bangs her head:
knocks pain into a cry.

She told me she saw you
in the thick of the following dawn
on the turn of her path.

Saw you in a grey suit
she'd never stroked straight before;
saw you brush the lemon balm;
heard you rustle the chinese lanterns
in the vase on the porch.

Standing by the back door
you lit a cigarette –
waiting.

She called out
but you'd gone –
your smoke left a milky halo
in her eyes.

The vicar came to pray.
We knelt on her carpet,
by her chair,
by her sideboard with your photo

always in the centre,
by the faded marzipan pear
in the clear plastic box
you'd bought her once.

Sometimes I dream that I go
into the old shed and find you
curled up in a corner.
You tell me that you fell
from the sky
unharmed, but dazed,
and have taken all these years
to come back to us.

I lead you confused
into the darkened room.

"THROWING THE LIGHTNESS
ON THESE THINGS"

It is no accident
that tonight as I pull you
from the turned debris of recollection
the baby cries, my daughter vomits –
my son pulls his comforting blanket
closer to his lips.

The last time I saw you
thick fog gauzed a screen between us
leaving the first months
of every year since
tight as TB
caught in my throat.
As the passenger
I had to lean out of the car door
to feel for the kerb in a foreign city
squinting for signs and junctions –
a scarf around my mouth.

*

I clutch my sister
pegging washing on the line.
We go in and watch
fragmented film footage of a forest
deflowered by stretchers and fuselage.

We wait by the Rayburn
for our parents
to come back from their bike ride.
How do you tell your father
his only brother is dead?

At 8 the next morning

the phone call confirming
and his cry
that had me running all the way round
the blind corner
going the long way back to school
where the headmaster sent me home again.

Past the village church
feeding stacks of flame into the sky –
the stained glass cracking
louder than crunched barley sugars.

*

This was not an over-six-foot-box.
I wondered which bits of you they'd got
or if they'd left anything behind
in the forest.
Maybe you were muddled up with someone else –
several people even.
I wondered if they'd arranged you nicely
or just slung everything in.
Perhaps you'd got shifted around on the journey –
all piled up at one end or one side.
Perhaps it was all a mistake
and you weren't there at all,
you'd got lost –
snagged in a tree
and you'd turn up one day
just like you always did
full of exciting new plans:
          "Throwing the Lightness on these things.
          Laughing it all away.
          Laughing it all away."

FUNERALE

the clear winds bring
a moment without rain

the padre's foot is in the mud
and his lace hem will be too
if he leans over –
he swings smoke
into the grave

the lid thuds
with little handfuls of clay –
clods that look as if
they'd come off a building site

I wanted to crumble mine
softly sprinkle it over you as
fine as parmesan from the silver bowl
on the silver spoon –
but it was sticky with stones
that clacked on the wood

cuddled as they were over the other side
but the wind at my back pulled
at my coat and kept my hands
in my pockets
it was right I should come alone

only 'Amen' only 'Amen'
the white choirboys and the nuns
in their brown gabardine

C'ERA UNA VOLTA
(Italian – 'Once upon a time'
pronounced – chaira oona volta)

Allora, allora.
I want to say –
c'era una volta.

You were little
in your Nonna's house
on the mountain.
They loved you,

sat you on the high stool
at the table and fed you
black fruit. You knew
how to spit the pip
into your neat fisted hand
and tip it into the saucer.

They watched you their
berry-brown lovely faces
in from the fields and
your Nonna slicing polenta –
each with a spoon
waiting for salsa.

Allora
c'era una volta

a tall woman with a big hat
is ordering jars in Fort*u*num and Mason,
as she always called it.
Jars for her tomato sauce
and spiced peppers.
She will line them up in the pantry,
sealed with olio
that she has shipped from Italy.

RARE SUBTERRANEAN FUNGI
(for B. and M.)

The proprietor comes to our table
with white truffles
in a locked Kilner jar:
he keeps them in a fridge
behind the bar.

He says,
"See what I have for you tonight,"
as he releases the lid.
The invisible cloud surrounds us
and we know this smell
for the first time:
inhaling the earthy nut aroma,
that Nonna told us about,
again and again.

At the base of his glass safe
rest three eggs
to absorb moisture.
Each of his rare fungi
is wrapped in Kleenex.

He lifts one out
as gently as if he held
a new-born round of life:
Tom Thumb or Thumbelina
that grew from mutated spores
among tree roots.

Unwrapping, with the gentlest
pinching back of its coverings,
he reveals its form.
"Here is my precious child
that I pay many lira
per kilo for."

He rocks it
from palm
to palm.

Found by a snouty dog or pig
that pressed the place;
teased out from its mouldy membranes
by a man with thick hands
and deep pockets.
This would have been early,
just on the dawn:
we can see the brown tinge
of first sun on its skin –
or are they the bruises
of confinement?

He rocks it
from palm
to palm.

Intoxicated we agree
to the sampling
of this delicacy.

The hot creamy risotto is served.
He flexes his arms
to show a crisp cuff –
then slides the white body
over his small silver slicer
leaving dry slivers of flesh
to flavour our food.

I'VE SEEN THE CHAMBERS

I've seen the chambers
of your heart –
clear islands
on a rare
hazeless day.

IN AN INTERIOR
(after Robert Campin)

She does not offer him her body as others do:
he observes her discreetly –
draws the child at her breast
rhythmically gripping the flesh.

He watches her peeling off his wet garments
sponging and drying his doughey body
with soft cottons draped over her knees.
The child giggles and squeals
when she makes deep growls, pretends to eat him –
lifts him high over her head – and down
to stand in the dip of her lap.

Quickly he sketches him:
sucking her chin, his right hand
touching his penis budding like a new pear,
then turning to smile.
Her eyes become milky.

The sun wakes the child with the birds.
He stands in his crib shouting –
muddling the blankets
making grooves in the wood with his new teeth.
She goes to him from the bed by the wall.
Knowing there is nothing to trip her
opens only half of one eye and undoes her shift –
lifts his jumping body into her side.
He presses his face to her neck –
opens his eyes wide.

She lays down drawing the warm covers over him.
His mouth knows the place.
His feet nudge the mat of her pubis
her hand cups his head.

FIRE

A quickening –
magnetic orange; always moving
as water; a blue stab wounding silence.

A sting in the eyes,
and even more so with touch,
as the darns in the muscles of my thighs
when the child was born.
A bursting of skins –

blackened chestnuts nuzzled out
smudged with white dust –
as sleepy badgers emerging from the set.

Every morning scooping
the slump of warm powder –
it still kindles
the smoothed papers
of Amaretti.

MY SLOW OPEN-TOP LIMOUSINE
(for Paul Durcan)

Walking
we drop down out of the wind
the wet walls wing us
in the silence. I show you how
the Himalayan Balsam flicks its seeds
with the lightest brush of my glove. Then
beat the empty galvanised tank
at the top of the path.

You scrumpling newspaper into your shoes
placing them on a log by the fire.
Then words pouring peace –
words that slip tiny newsprint
ticker-taping
ticker-taping
my slow open-top limousine –
my bare arms lifted
up.

EVE TO MICHELANGELO

The sticky halt of skin creating skin:
your hand, that inked our initial lives into cartoons,
will sweep our naked bodies across a heaven within.
We are suspended, framed by spandrel and cornice.

In pestle and mortar you pound colour to dust:
mix and apply, blocking us in with broad strokes. You have
chosen to tuck me under God's gentle arm where I must
watch Him make man with a touch.

You have shielded the light and dark folds of me behind Him.
Now, do not give me a timorous look, as I espy
this Adam, but paint apprehension in my eyes and see
that my brow shows an awakening of curiosity.

SHUTTING DOWN THE CRYSTAL FURNACE

It is crystal glass I want to write about.
Not the precious remainders of hand cut sets
from the family hotel in Marina di Massa
some with their stems superglued
or the boxed ranges you have in the cellar,
on the top ledges of the kitchen,
or the ranks in the glazed cabinet
with their labels unpeeled
or the droplets and baubles
from unstrung chandeliers
you have wrapped in cloth bags

but the white molten glass
you have shown me
through eye-drying spy holes.

Molten glass I've watched you poke out in gobs
like bloody toffee on apples –
the strands crackling
brittle out of the batch.

Molten glass from temperamental furnaces
that have always caused problems.

Molten glass that erupts and froths
when the mix is wrong
extruding faults and seeds
in the final mouldings.

As now
agitating the phone lines from Tuscany to Essex
to have you 'pronto' solutions in your mother tongue
on the piano stool in the hallway
momentarily shushing the grandchildren
mimicking perfectly

whilst rolling round your feet.

As always
I listen from the kitchen and have never understood
but feel all the words bubbling through me
only to catch in the back of my throat
like static amoeba in the displayed goblet –
trapped in leaden crystal
that cannot be fluted.

Later, over pasta,
you explain the physics in detail:
how some bloke banged the feeder with his hammer
before he clocked off from the weekend shift
and the excess side siltings of silica
fed into the furnace
which frothed up on Tuesday.

You told them
to shut it down –
brick it up.

LA FONTANA DI TREVI

Dressed for the heat, map in my hand,
in alleys searching for the Trevi fountain –
I listen for direction
but stumble upon it drained and mute.
It is criss-crossed and screened
with scaffold and blue awnings.
Men in loose black trousers
with gold necklaces and gold shoulders
offer models of Neptune in all sizes.
Wanting my coins their eyes dip deep
with the quick cool dark air before thunder.
I shelter in the arcade of a shoe shop
as they weight large plastic sheets
over Colosseums and wolves suckling boy-twins.
They stand sharing cigarettes in doorways opposite.
The road between us is loud with white-water –
the downpour snatching my breath.

SUMMER EXHIBITION

Try this for starters:
'Fever' playing on the station radio
when you buy your return.
And when you pull in at his station
you press and push down the window
wave his attention, just like the films, and wait
with a flicked book in your lap, lifting your eyes
until he fills the space that's beside you.

Later, with your stomach surging
as if in a fast lift ascending,
you view pictures apart, but brushing and bumping
like dodgems that can't help but make contact.
You whisper of halved lemons in muslin
through the pulsed hum of fans
and dip your hands into fountains
while the tar melts love into too loose a word
ticking the grit around tyre treads.
You're saying "Can you live without it?
The most memorable...
The images you're left with..."

The falling of night then and the journey back?
Try this: in an open compartment
you let your head fall to his shoulder
sleep flirts with your eyelids so that dreamlike
the woman in a strappy red dress down the carriage
slips off her shoes, curls in her lover's lap
while he rests his bike magazine on her hip
his pages doubled back round the spine
and you want them to kiss, want her to
lift her hem as his magazine slips to the floor –
and you watch for her breasts and her toes.

You feel his thumb run your spine

like a spurt of blue water –
and you'll step out the door in the morning
tipping tea leaves onto the earth
having had no sleep without him
wanting to slip out with a blanket –
to take him on a hilltop.
Honeysuckle scent marinades the ache
your favourite rose has exploded
into its first bloom of summer
and the seeds that you sprinkled last week
have broken the surface with their frecklings of leaves.
Sudden rain steams up the tarmac as if newly rollered.
Your friend recommends a book she's been reading
'Feel the fear, and do it anyway'.
Your students are jotting notes on a video
you're saying "Does it do anything for you?
If it makes you cry say why."
Robert De Niro saying "Anything's possible"
as you press 'stop' and rewind it.
And neither of you will remember where he left his Times.

ON ENTERING HIS HOUSE

The burglar alarm off
she goes through the double glazed doors
turns the rattly brass handle ridged like a beehive.
She has dreamt of this vestibule –
this openness – the other rooms in this house.

He is the wide magnificient floor
spilling its apron from the ribbon of stairs.
She lets her feet slide into V-ing diagonals
as she had once skated through the British Museum.
She needs no permission –
she feels the firm level of him and then
she remembers the stirring – the gutsy excitement
of spaces she remembers how to tip herself
upside down into handstands – yes – her skirt
scalloped into her knicker-legs – ten seconds
maybe ten seconds upside upside down with her palms
on his warm shiny surface twisting down then back up
with a hop leaning into a wall her rib cage protruding
her red face counting potatoes.

And then she remembers she could never do cartwheels
never felt herself into the consecutive tumblings
like the girls that rode the bus home with a ha'p'ny
and played up the Pleasure Pit.
She knows – knows the one.two.three.four. pattern
that can rotate her sideways and feels him
sensing her patterning sensing
the multiple blur in her head. He gently shifts her
as a hairbreadth of earthquake
the small unsettling of a block of loose parquet
a sudden pool of red light – and she raises
her knee to a skip raises her arms over her head
as she marks the diagonal with five spirographic
arcs of her body as a child's helix petals

on a vast bowing flower
rolls as a surfer with no allusions to footholds.
Mid-tumble – mid-circle she shouts it – shouts it
out loud – and the rest – all of it –
there –
she's said it…

He gives her his hand – his smooth honey polish
you could tie a bow tie in – he gives her
his hand – his unmanicured hand.
She puts her mouth to the traces of earth
in his broken nails – tastes the salt – hears
its grit like swishing skates in a warm-up.

IF I LIVED IN ITALY

If I lived in Italy I would walk
in the early morning cool of gullied streets
zoccoli echoing between the machine stitch of mopeds
my hair simply swept from the back of my neck
with a tortoiseshell clip. Swinging my basket
into the shops – they'd know me here –
we'd talk aches bambini politica while I buy
focaccia carciofi parmigiano olio.

If I lived in Italy I would argue
over the table with you about anything:
slapping my forehead dismissively
pinching my fingers in emphasis
eating spaghetti with the speed of whisking –
using the serviette
as if I were splashing water on my face.

Every siesta we'd make love in fluent Italian
there would be no rush in the heat –
three hours today tomorrow the next day.
There would be no end to the cicala chorus
and sleep would be easy
having nowhere to go to but here.

If I lived in Italy I would throw words with my hands
as if releasing dove after dove.